Space and Alien Jokes That Are Out of This World

by Dianne Woo

Illustrated by Jack White

A TOM DOHERTY ASSOCIATES BOOK
NEW YORK

First published 1993 as a Tor Book by
Tom Doherty Associates, Inc., New York
First published in Great Britain in 1994 by Pan Books,
a division of Macmillan General Books
Cavaye Place London SW10 9PG
and Basingstoke

Associated companies throughout the world

ISBN 0 330 33976 1

Copyright © RGA Publishing Group, Inc., 1993
Art by Jack White

9 8 7 6 5 4 3 2 1

A CIP catalogue record for this book is available from
the British Library

Printed and bound in Great Britain by
Cox & Wyman Ltd, Reading, Berkshire

Why did the silly man throw a plate into the air?
  He wanted to see a flying saucer.

What did the astronaut feed his dog?
  Gravity Train.

When was beefsteak at its highest?
  When the cow jumped over the moon.

Where was the two-headed Martian queen crowned?
    On her heads.

Why can't the world ever come to an end?
    Because it is round.

Martian: Pardon me, earthling. How do we get to the White House?
Earthling: You have to campaign for it just like everyone else.

After the rocket ship took off for the moon, the captain told the passengers: "Ladies and gentlemen, the weather is good, we have excellent visibility, and we are proceeding on schedule. Unfortunately, we are lost!"

Alien: On this planet, earthling, we drive very unusual invisible cars.
Astronaut: What's so unusual about an invisible car?
Alien: You don't see one every day.

What cartoons do alien children like to watch?
  Lunar Tunes.

Two men were driving to Cape Kennedy for their first trip to Mars. "I wish we had brought the television with us," one of the men said. "What do you mean? We won't be able to get any TV programs on Mars, anyway," said the other. "I know," answered the first. "But our tickets were on it."

Venusian King: Agent 406, what did you bring back
   from earth?
Venusian agent: I bought this dog for $500. The
   earthling said it was part collie and part bull.
Venusian king: Which part is bull?
Venusian agent: I think it was the part about the
   $500.

What do aliens eat?
   Lunarfish sandwiches.

*What do aliens drink with their lunarfish
sandwiches?*
   Craterade.

*What do you call a Martian who drives her
spaceship perfectly?*
   A wreckless driver.

Alien king: And how was the weather on earth,
   agent Gorp?
Gorp: Well, the sky was clearer in New York than it
   was in London.
Alien king: And why was that?
Gorp: More skyscrapers, I suppose.

How did the sick astronaut get to the hospital?
   Flu.

A Venusian was sent on a mission to earth. When he arrived, he looked for an apartment to live in. A landlord showed him a very small, very dirty apartment. "How do you like this apartment as a whole?" the landlord asked. "As a hole it's all right," the Venusian answered, "but as an apartment it's terrible."

Why do Martians take baths in Tide?
    Because it's too cold out-tide.

Teacher: Class, what is a vacuum in space?
Student: I can't think of it just now, but it's in my
        head.

What do you call an alien with acne?
    Crater face.

What did the love-sick astronaut say to the cute ground control person?
    "You send me."

If you stand outside a spaceship to look through a telescope, what should you watch?
    Your step.

What do you call a blemish in space?
    A black hole.

Boy: What happened with the alien who had his head near a fireplace and his feet in a bucket of ice water?

Girl: I don't know, but on the average he was comfortable.

Two aliens landed on earth and had just eaten two entire garbage cans. "Wasn't that delicious?" asked one alien, to which the other alien replied, "That crust was good, but the filling was too rich."

1st astronaut: Are you a light sleeper?

2nd astronaut: No, I sleep in the dark.

Why did the moon go to the bank?
To change quarters.

Martian wife: Why are you putting that 25-watt light bulb into the socket?

Martian husband: The doctor told me to take a little light exercise.

Andrew alien: I crossed the Jupiter Sea twice and never took a bath.

Amy alien: You dirty double-crosser!

Why is the metric system confusing to aliens?
They can't make heads or tails of it, and it has no feet.

What did one Saturnian say to the other as they approached earth?
    "You'll like this place. It has atmosphere."

    Two astronauts were nervous about their first flight into space.
1st astronaut: Do you know the meaning of fear?
2nd astronaut: I'm afraid to ask.

What do you get when you cross a space computer with a crab?
    A machine that makes snappy decisions.

Why were the aliens showing films underwater?
    They wanted to go to a dive-in movie.

Little boy: How do spaceships stay in the air?
Father: I don't know.
Little boy: What do they use for fuel?
Father: I don't know.
Little boy: Does it bother you when I ask all these
    questions?
Father: Not at all, son. If you don't ask questions,
    how will you learn anything?

What do you call a Martian who eats her parents?
    An orphan.

Two Saturnians landed on earth and visited a museum. They saw a mummy in a glass case.
1st Saturnian: It says "1300 B.C." on the bottom of that mummy case. What do you think that means?
2nd Saturnian: It must be the license number of the car that hit him.

1st Neptunian: You've got your socks on the wrong feet.
2nd Neptunian: But these are the only feet I have.

When astronauts first landed on the moon, where did they stand?
   On their feet.

What's the fastest way to get to the moon?
   Crawl into an elephant's trunk and tickle him.

Who was the first person in space?
   The man in the moon.

Why is the planet Neptune like Mickey Mouse?
   Because it's close to Pluto.

1st astronaut: I see spots every time I go on a space
       flight.
2nd astronaut: Have you seen a doctor?
1st astronaut: No, just spots.

Teacher: Class, did you know that light travels from
       the sun to the earth at a speed of 186,000
       miles per second?
Student: So what? It's downhill all the way.

   A Neptunian arrived on earth with a painful
toothache. She immediately went into a dentist's
office. "Please check my teeth," she told the
dentist. "Why?" asked the dentist. "Don't you want
to keep them white?"

An alien was carrying a sign that read, "Beware!"
The end of the moon is coming."

Teacher: What is a satellite?
Student: It's what a cowboy puts on his horse at
    night.

1st alien: Did you hear about the Martian who
    bleached her hair?
2nd alien: No, what about her?
1st alien: Forget it, I never tell off-color stories.

What's the loudest thing in space?
    Shooting stars.

1st Saturnian: Which travels faster, heat or cold?
2nd Saturnian: Heat. You can catch a cold easily.

*What do you call an asteroid that gives parking
tickets?*
    A meteor maid.

Teacher: What was the name of the first satellite to
    orbit the earth?
Student: The moon.

What do you do if a Martian swallows a roll of film?
    Wait and see what develops.

1st alien: I admire your new furniture.
2nd alien: Thank you. It's Earthly American style.

What do astronauts eat in space?
  Neptuna casseroles.

Why was the baby raised on Martian milk?
  He was a baby Martian.

1st astronaut: When did you become a sky diver?
2nd astronaut: When the spaceship caught fire.

Martian leader: Agent Zondar, what did you
    discover during your trip to Europe?
Zondar: In Spain, the favorite sport is bullfighting. In
    England, it is cricket. I would prefer to play in
    England.
Martian leader: What makes you say that?
Zondar: It is easier to fight crickets.

What do Martians play at parties?
  Moon-opoly.

*Why did the alien beekeeper cross his bees with
lightning bugs?*
  So they could work at night.

Annie: Have they figured out where the universe
    ends yet?
Fannie: No. It's still up in the air.

What do aliens like on their hot chocolate?
  Mars-mallows.

What does an astronaut write on?
  A launching pad.

Two astronauts were getting ready for blast-off.

1st astronaut: Darn! I forgot my gloves again.

2nd astronaut: Why didn't you tie a string around your finger?

1st astronaut: Well, to tell you the truth, my gloves are warmer.

What's an astronaut's favorite food?
  Meteor loaf.

How does Obi-Wan Kenobi get from one place to another?
  Ewoks. (He walks.)

Who is married to Darth Vader?
  Ella Vader.

What's a toad's favorite science fiction film?
  Star Warts.

What fish is a space hero?
  Fluke Skywalker.

What happens when Darth Vader misses three pitches?
  The empire strikes out.

What's soft, red, and wears a black helmet?
  Darth Tomato.

Why couldn't the Martian banker ride a bicycle anymore?
She lost her balance.

An alien ordered a salad at a restaurant. When the waiter brought it, the alien saw a button in the bowl. "Waiter," he said, "there's a button in my salad!" "Oh, don't worry, sir," the waiter said. "It probably fell off while the salad was dressing."

An insomniac alien landed on earth and went to see a doctor.
Alien: Doctor, I can't sleep at night.
Doctor: Did you try counting sheep?
Alien: Yes, I counted up to 200,000.
Doctor: My goodness! Then you fell asleep?
Alien: No, then it was time to get up.

Teacher: What does it mean when the barometer starts falling?
Student: Whoever nailed it to the wall didn't do a good job.

What does an astronaut use to carry his sandwich?
A launchpail.

What do you call an insect space hero?
Bug Rogers.

An astronaut landed on Saturn but forgot to bring his wallet with him. He went into a Saturnian bank. "I need to borrow some money," he told the alien clerk. 'I'm sorry," said the clerk, "but the loan arranger isn't in today." "That's all right," said the astronaut, "I'll talk to Tonto instead."

What do werewolves do in space?
Moonlight.

What word describes a spaceship about to launch and Dracula when he's not feeling well?
Countdown.

Why is a witch like a UFO?
She is a flying sorceress.

What does an astronaut take off last before going into suspended animation?
He takes his feet off the floor.

What happened to the rocket scientist who fell into acid?
She got absorbed in her work.

Why did the silly astronaut join the army?
He wanted to be a real space cadet.

When is coffee like the surface of the earth?
When it is ground.

Did you hear about the silly astronaut?
He tried to fill in a black hole.

Two Plutonians were in a bookstore on earth.
1st Plutonian: This book is marvelous! It hasn't got much of a plot, but what a cast!
2nd Plutonian: That's a telephone book you're reading.

If athletes get athlete's foot, what do astronauts get?
  Missile toe.

If athletes get athlete's foot and astronauts get
missile toe, what does a moon surveyor get?
  Two square feet.

Astronaut: May day! I'm low on oxygen. I have only
59 seconds left.
Ground control: Sorry, we can't hear you. We're
getting interference. Just give us a minute . . .

*What would you do if you floated out to space on
an iceberg?*
Keep cool until you are rescued.

*Why is Saturn like a person who has been engaged
several times?*
Both have many rings.

1st Martian: What are an earthling's three favorite
words?
2nd Martian: I don't know.
1st Martian: That's correct.

1st astronaut: My foot falls asleep and wakes me up
every night.
2nd astronaut: How can it wake you up if it's
asleep?
1st astronaut: It snores.

Mother: If you look up in the sky, Billy, you can see
the man in the moon.
Billy: Doesn't he want to come down?

1st alien: Don't drive so close to the edge of the crater. I'm getting dizzy.

2nd alien: Don't be such a chicken. Just close your eyes. That's what I'm doing.

What did the Martian say when he took apart his robot?
   "Well . . . rust in peace."

1st Martian: Why are you saluting that refrigerator from earth?

2nd Martian: Because it's a General Electric.

A woman was traveling on a rocket ship for the first time. When she heard the engine start up, she closed her eyes and nervously held onto the arms of her seat. Then she opened her eyes and looked out the window. "Look at those tiny people down there," she commented to her husband. "They look just like ants!" "Those *are* ants, dear," he said. "We haven't left the ground yet."

Teacher: Class, heat expands, cold contracts. Can anyone give me an example?

Student: Sure. Hot summer days are long, cold winter days are short.

Mary: That model rocket in the museum is missing!
Larry: Really?
Mary: Yes. In its place was a card that read:
    "Farewell, earthlings."

A bum settled down near the Washington Monument and started a fire at the base to cook his dinner. Another bum walked by, looked at the fire and the shape of the monument, and said, "You'll never get it off the ground."

What do you get if you cross an alien with a skunk?
  Something that stinks to high heaven.

What's fast and goes "MOOZ"?
  A rocket ship flying backward.

Astronaut: Every time I go into space, I just gaze out
    the window and watch the sun rise.
Reporter: That's nothing. I can just stay home and
    watch the kitchen sink.

Astronaut: I feel funny after that last space trip,
    doctor. What should I do?
Doctor: Go on television.

1st Saturnian: (surveying earth from spaceship):
    What do you think of Red China?
2nd Saturnian: It depends on the color of the
    tablecloth.

  Two Alpha Centaurians were walking down
a city street.
1st Centaurian: Ouch! I just stepped on a pin.
2nd Centaurian: It's OK. It's a safety pin.

Teacher: Who can tell me what the sun is made of?
Student: It's made of helium.
Teacher: What makes you say that?
Student: It rises every day, doesn't it?

Martian: What does the X-ray of my head show?
Doctor: Nothing:

1st alien: Where were you born?
2nd alien: Jupiter.
1st alien: Which part?
2nd alien: All of me, silly.

1st astronaut: What do you get if you cross a rocket
    scientist with a rubber band?
2nd astronaut: I don't know, what?
1st astronaut: I don't know what it's called, but it
    makes snap decisions.

Just before the Alpha Centaurian left earth for
her home planet, she stopped at a drugstore.
"Please give me a box of talcum power," she said.
"Certainly," the clerk answered. "Would you like it
scented?" "No," the Centaurian responded, "I'll
take it with me."

A Martian walked into a soda shoppe and
ordered a hot fudge sundae. The clerk brought him
the sundae. When the Martian finished eating it, he
gave the clerk a $20 bill. The clerk thought the
Martian did not know anything about earth money,
so she gave the Martian one dollar in change.
"Hope you liked the sundae," she told the Martian.
"We don't get very many Martians like you in
here." "No wonder," said the Martian. "At $19 a
sundae, I'm surprised anyone would come in here."

What happened to the Neptunian after he was run
over by a tractor?
    Nothing. He just lay there with a long face.

Why is being an astronaut a backward job?
  You have to be fired before you can work.

What do you call the person who pushes the button to fire the rockets?
  Sir Launchalot.

*What happened when the rocket scientist mixed
poison ivy with a four-leaf clover?*
    She had a rash of good luck.

Martian: I would like to buy a bus ticket to New
    York City, please.
Ticket seller: Would you like to go by Buffalo?
Martian: Don't be silly, earthling. I would like to go
    by bus.

1st alien: How did you find the weather when you
    were on earth?
2nd alien: Simple. I just went outside, and there it
    was.

Teacher: Suzie, what is a comet?
Suzie: I don't know.
Teacher: Don't you know what you call a star with
    a tail?
Suzie: Oh, sure. Mickey Mouse.

Why do hippies like to study the stars?
    Because they're so far-out.

*How can you tell if there's a 30-foot alien under
your bed?*
    Your nose will be pressed against the ceiling.

1st Martian: I complimented my girlfriend and now
    she's mad at me.
2nd Martian: I thought I told you to tell her that
    when you look into her eyes, time stands still.
1st Martian: Well, I didn't say exactly that.
2nd Martian: What did you say?
1st Martian: I told her that she had a face that
    would stop a clock.

Why did the astronaut go to bed?
    Because the bed wouldn't come to her.

Ground control: When you land on Mercury, you'll
    be greeted by one of the planet's inhabitants.
    He's 12 inches tall, but don't laugh at him.
Astronaut: Why:
Ground control: We've been informed that he's a
    ruler.

A Plutonian joined a basketball team on earth,
but he never got to play. One day he brought a gun
to the game. "Why do you have a gun?" asked
another player. "The coach said I'd finally get to
shoot the ball tonight," the Plutonian said proudly.

Teacher: Class, who can tell me what an atom is?
Student: Isn't he the dude who went with Eve?

What's the difference between the rising sun and the setting sun?
   The whole world.

1st Venusian: Did you take a bath today?
2nd Venusian: Why, is there one missing?

Alien mom: Who gave you that black eye?
Alien kid: No one. I had to fight for it.

What holds up the sun?
   Sun beams.

   Two astronauts were preparing for the shuttle launch.
1st astronaut: I have butterflies in my stomach.
2nd astronaut: Did you try taking an aspirin?
1st astronaut: I did, and the butterflies started playing tennis with it.

What eye makeup do aliens use?
   Mars-cara.

What did the metric Martian say?
   "Take me to your liter.

How did the metric Martian make coffee?
   With a percoliter. (percolator)

29

A monkey and an astronaut were sent up in a space shuttle. The monkey received the following instructions over the comlink: "Collect rock samples. Test zero gravity. Monitor satellite readings . . . " The list went on, and the astronaut became upset. "Hey, what am I supposed to do?" he asked ground control. "You feed the monkey," was the answer.

1st astronaut: My space shuttle ran over a duckway
    last night.
2nd astronaut: What's a duckway?
1st astronaut: Oh, about five pounds.

What do you call a rare alien?
    An endangered space-ies.

Why did the alien baker stop making doughnuts?
    She was tired of the hole business.

1st astronaut: I don't feel so well after that last flight.
    I think I'm coming down with snoo.
2nd astronaut: What's snoo?
1st astronaut: Not much. What's new with you?

1st alien: What do you see when the smog clears in
    Los Angeles?
2nd alien: I don't know, what?
1st alien: UCLA.

Judge: I can't send this Martian to prison. He's deaf.
Attorney: Pardon me, sir, but what difference does
    that make?
Judge: I can't sentence anyone to jail without a
    hearing.

1st astronaut: An alien panhandler came up to me and asked me for a dollar to eat.
2nd astronaut: Did you give one to him?
1st astronaut: Yes, and he ate it.

Astronaut: Ever since that last space flight, I've had trouble breathing.
Doctor: We'll find a way to stop that.

Sal: Did you get a hold of anyone at Cape Kennedy?
Hal: No. They were all out to launch.

Andy: Hey, I heard you want to be an astronaut. Do you wanna fly?
Candy: Yes, I do.
Andy: Well, hold on a minute, and I'll catch one for you.

Teacher: Everyone who would like to go into space, raise your hands. (Everyone raises their hands except Johnny.) Johnny, you don't want to go into space?
Johnny: I do, but my mom said I have to come straight home after school.

Why is a cat like the sun?
    They both go out at night.

Why did the silly astronaut use cake to clean up his spilled milk?

It was a pound cake.

What do you call a young Russian child who goes into space?

A cosmotot.

What did the alien plant in his backyard?
  A rock garden

Teacher: Class, the law of gravity keeps us on earth.
Student: So what did people do before the law was
    passed?

1st astronaut: Why did you get rid of your space
    suit? It fit you like a glove!
2nd astronaut: That's the problem. It should fit me
    like a space suit.

1st astronaut: What did you get the little medal for?
2nd astronaut: For singing.
1st astronaut: What did you get the big medal for?
2nd astronaut: For stopping.

Why did the astronaut start looking like an antenna?
   He ate too many TV dinners.

What did the alien say when he saw the garbage can fall off the garbage truck?
   "Ma'am! You dropped your purse!"

What did the Martian say when he walked into the bar and saw a jukebox?
   "What's a nice girl like you doing in a place like this?"

How did Bugs Bunny get to the moon?
   By rabbit transit.

What did the alien say when he unplugged his robot?
   "AC come, AC go."

What's the difference between a space monster and a doughnut?
   You can dunk a doughnut in your coffee.

Assistant: Mr. President, Senator Qu'ryl'lian'no'allax'ia
      from Mars is on his way here.
President: How do you spell that?
Assistant: M-A-R-S.

Two Plutonians were in New York City.
"Where's the park?" one said. "There isn't one
here," said the other. "Then why does that sign say
'Park Here'?" said the first.

1st astronaut: There's an alien outside with a metal
    leg named Klaxon.
2nd astronaut: What's the name of his other leg?

Two Martians were eating at a restaurant on
earth. "Something must be wrong with these
oysters. I've eaten 12 and I've got a stomach ache,"
said one Martian. "Are they fresh? How did they
look when you opened the shells?" asked the other
Martian. "You're supposed to open the shells?"
answered the first Martian.

What do Plutonians call little black dogs?
    Puppies.

1st astronaut: There was a big noise this morning.
2nd astronaut: Was it the crack of dawn?
1st astronaut: No, it was the break of day.

Mrs. Martian: I baked three kinds of mooncakes
    today, dear. Would you like to take your pick?
Mr. Martian: No, I'll just use my hammer.

Why did the bees go into space?
They were on their honeymoon.

How do you get an alien out of a bathtub?
Pull out the plug.

1st Venusian: After my trip to an earth farm, I
learned one thing.
2nd Venusian: What's that?
1st Venusian: Never try to milk a bull.

Earthling: Did you lose something?
Alien: Yes, I dropped my watch.
Earthling: Where did you drop it?
Alien: On 24th Street.
Earthling: But this is 27th Street!
Alien: Well, when I dropped it, it was still running.

Where do they make wine in space?
  On the Planet of the Grapes.

What do construction workers drive in space?
  Star trucks.

What do merchants sell in outer space?
  Star wares.

What space hero has only one hand?
  Hand Solo.

What's brown, wears a black helmet, and makes good french fries?
  Darth Tater.

What's green and uses the Force?
  Leek Skywalker.

A tailor looked out of his shop window and saw a spaceship land. Three aliens got out and started walking toward his store. One had three heads, the second had eight eyes, and the third had sixteen arms. "Quick!" he told his assistant. "Take down the sign that says, 'Free Alterations'!"

1st scientist: We have a new computer to help us with space travel. It's very intelligent.
2nd scientist: Why is it so intelligent?
1st scientist: Well, I just gave it a problem to solve, and it asked for a raise.

1st astronaut: Well, we've crash-landed on this unknown planet. What do we do now?
2nd astronaut: Let's think a moment.
1st astronaut: No, let's do something you can do, too.

The president of the United States was interviewing an alien who had just landed on earth.
President: Where were you born?
Alien: On Pluto.
President: Why were you born on Pluto?
Alien: Because I wanted to be near my mother.

What's a baseball player's favorite science fiction film?
  The Umpire Strikes Back.

When do Martians go to school?
  From Moonday through Saturnday.

Italian chef: How do our Italian dishes compare to
    your Venusian ones?
Venusian customer: Oh, they break just as easily.

What do you call a branch of the alien military?
  The Space-ial forces.

1st astronaut: On my last trip into space, I lived on a
jar of peanut butter for a month.
2nd astronaut: What kept you from falling off?

*What did the rocket scientist say when his computer
calculated the correct answer?*
  "Data boy."

1st astronaut: Why are you always carrying that
    rabbits foot around?
2nd astronaut: To keep the aliens away.
1st astronaut: But there aren't any aliens for miles
    around!
2nd astronaut: See? It works!

Reporter: What is your secret for surviving so long
in outer space?
Astronaut: I eat a head of garlic six times a day.
Reporter: And you're able to keep that a secret?

*Who made the first space shuttle that didn't get off
the ground?*
The Wrong Brothers.

How do astronauts sleep?
  With their eyes closed.

Astronaut: Doctor, I always get sick the day before a
    spaceflight.
Doctor: Why don't you try leaving a day earlier?

Where did the alien cook get her seasonings?
  From her space rack.

Why did the alien finally take a bath?
  He decided to give up a life of grime.

What do you do with a green alien?
  See if he's ripe.

  A Cape Kennedy technician called to check on
the weather for the upcoming launch.
Technician: Hello, is this the Weather Bureau?
Weather Bureau: Yes, it is.
Technician: Can we expect a shower today?
Weather Bureau: Well, it's OK with us. Take one if
    you want to.

1st astronaut: My toaster broke the other day, so I
    fixed it with some old spaceship parts.
2nd astronaut: Does it work OK?
1st astronaut: Yes, except when the toast pops up,
    it circles the table twice before landing.

What started the fight on the passenger spaceship?
  The conductor punched the tickets.

Why does an alien monster sleep all day?
  Who'd want to wake it up?

Tracy: How much is the moon worth?
Stacey: A dollar, because it has four quarters.

What dish is absolutely out of this world?
  A flying saucer.

Boy: There's going to be an eclipse today. Do you
    want to watch it with me?
Girl: OK. What channel is it on?

What is an alien after she's 10 years old?
  11 years old.

1st Venusian: Why are you eating that banana with
    the peel still on?
2nd Venusian: It's all right. I know what's inside.

Why was the alien bashful?
  He went into the closet every time he changed
his mind.

What did the girl alien say to the boy alien?
"I want to hold your hand, hand, hand, hand."

1st astronaut: Where were you born?
2nd astronaut: In a hospital.
1st astronaut: What was wrong with you?

What happened when the Martian cowgirl spilled root beer on her stove?

She had foam on the range.

Why did the astronaut take quarters to bed?
   They were his sleeping quarters.

After months in space, what finally brings an astronaut back to earth?
   Gravity.

What does an astronaut eat off of?
   A satellite dish.

What does an astronaut do when she gets mad?
   She blasts off.

What sentence did the Martian get for robbing the lamp store?
   50 light years.

Why did the astronaut put iodine on his paycheck?
   He got a cut in his salary.

1st Plutonian: Hey, be careful with that ray gun. You just missed shooting me.
2nd Plutonian: Did I? I'm sorry. I won't miss next time.

What happened when the bald man saw the alien?
   It was a hair-raising experience.

What do rocket scientists do at Christmas?
  Kiss under the missile-toe.

1st astronaut: Our computer isn't working again!
    Where did the programmer go?
2nd astronaut: She went data way.

Why were E.T.'s eyes so big?
He saw his phone bill.

What happened when E.T. put too much detergent in the dishwasher?
E.T. foam home.

An alien on earth was approached by a panhandler. "I haven't had a meal in three days," the panhandler pleaded. "Oh, my," the alien replied, "I wish I had your will power!"

What kind of spaceship is always saying it's sorry?
An Apollo G.

An astronaut lived on dehydrated food for one month while he was aboard a space shuttle. When he returned to earth, he was caught in a bad rainstorm. It took him a few minutes to get out of the rain, but he gained 100 pounds in the process!

1st Martian: I just flew in from Pluto.
2nd Martian: Your arms must be tired.

What travels around the earth without using any gasoline?
The moon.

An astronaut had just returned from a mission to Saturn.

Reporter: Ma'am, what do the inhabitants of Saturn
  eat?
Astronaut: Anything they can find.
Reporter: And what if they can't find anything?
Astronaut: Then they eat something else.

An alien had just landed on earth when he was approached by a beggar. "Could you give me a couple of dollars for a sandwich?" the beggar asked. "I don't know," said the alien. "Let me see the sandwich first."

1st alien: What are you doing?
2nd alien: I'm writing a letter to my brother on
  Pluto.
1st alien: But you don't know how to write.
2nd alien: That's OK. My brother doesn't know
  how to read.

Shelly: What happened to that astronaut you were
  dating?
Kelly: We broke up. He wasn't right for me.
Shelly: Why?
Kelly: I'm looking for someone who is more down
  to earth.

Why did the astronaut wear a bulletproof vest?
  To protect himself from shooting stars.

What did the alien eat after he had his teeth pulled?
  The dentist.

Patty: What happens when the sun comes out at
    night?
Matty: Oh, that'll be the day.

What do you do with a blue Alpha Centaurian?
  Cheer it up.

  Said one laboratory rat to the other: "I think I've
got this researcher conditioned. He gives me some
cheese every time I go through the maze."

1st Martian: I had an embarrassing experience
    when I was on earth.
2nd Martian: What happened?
1st Martian: I opened a refrigerator and saw a
    Russian dressing.

  An impatient alien went into a restaurant for
breakfast. "I want some pancakes," he ordered.
"Will they be long?" "No, sir, round," answered
the waiter.

1st astronaut: I feel sick after orbiting so much. Call
    me a doctor.
2nd astronaut: OK, you're a doctor.

*What happened when the spaceship carrying 200
boomerangs blasted off toward the moon?*
  It took off, then came back again, then took off,
then came back again . . .

1st Venusian: Did you hear what happened to Zog when he was on a farm on earth? He got hurt while taking a milk bath.
2nd Venusian: How could he get hurt by milk?
1st Venusian: The cow fell on him.

Lost Martian: Pardon me, earthling. Where does this road lead to?
Hillbilly: Cain't say I know.
Lost Martian: Well, how about that other road? Where does it lead to?
Hillbilly: Cain't say I know that either.
Lost Martian: You're not very smart, are you?
Hillbilly: I wouldn't say that. I'm not the one who's lost.

1st astronaut: Give me that potfer.
2nd astronaut: What's a potfer?
1st astronaut: To cook in, silly.

1st Neptunian: We must find a place to land on
earth. Where is the English Channel?
2nd Neptunian: I don't know. It's not on our TV.

*Why did the astronaut have to go to the hospital
after a tomato fell on his head?*
Because it was in a can.

Why didn't the Martian cross the road?
She didn't want to be mistaken for a chicken.

What happened after the moon ate a big meal?
It was a full moon.

1st astronaut: What's the difference between
lightning and electricity?
2nd astronaut: Lightning is free.

The space station hired a consultant to help them
with a scientific problem. The consultant said that
she would charge $500 to answer two questions.
"Isn't that rather expensive?" the head of the space
station asked. "I don't think it is," the consultant
replied. "Now what is your second question?"

Why can't an elephant become an astronaut?
Because there isn't a space suit big enough to fit him.

Shuttle pilot: Ladies and gentlemen, you are inside the most advanced space shuttle ever built. We are flying through space faster than any human being has flown before.

Passengers: Wonderful!

Shuttle pilot: There is one problem, though.

Passengers: What's that?

Shuttle pilot: I have no idea where we're going.

Teacher: If we breathe oxygen in the daytime, what do we breathe at night?

Student: Nitrogen.

Teacher: Class, who can name four shooting stars?

Billy: Annie Oakley, Wild Bill Hickok, Jesse James, and Billy the Kid.

Two Saturnians landed in London.

1st Saturnian: This has got to be the foggiest place on earth.

2nd Saturnian: No, it isn't. I've been to a city that's even foggier.

1st Saturnian: What city was that?

2nd Saturnian: I don't know. It was too foggy to tell.

Did you hear about the thousand-year-old egg they found on the moon?
   Never mind, it's an old yolk.

1st alien: Now that we've landed on earth, I'm
       hungry. Let's eat up the street.
2nd alien: No, thanks. I don't like the taste of
       asphalt.

*What do rocket mechanics give each other on
Valentine's Day?*
    Forget-me-nuts.

Space police: I stopped you because you were
      going the wrong way down a one-way street.
      Didn't you see the arrow?
Space pilot: To tell you the truth, sir, I didn't even
      see the Indians.

What happened to the clumsy astronaut?
  He tripped over a black hole.

Benny: Are you tan from the sun?
Jenny: No, I'm Jenny from the earth.

Teacher: Johnny, please recite the alphabet.
Johnny: A, B, C, D, F, G, H, I, J, K, L, M, N, O, P,
    Q, R, S, U, V, W, X, Y, Z.
Teacher: But what happened to E, T?
Johnny: Oh, he went home.

Two Plutonians were in a laundromat.
1st Plutonian: You know, earth television is not as
    bad as everyone says.
2nd Plutonian: That's a clothes dryer you're
    watching.

Astronaut: Doctor, will I be able to fly a space
    shuttle after this cast comes off my arm?
Doctor: Why, certainly.
Astronaut: Good! I've never been able to fly a
    shuttle before.

Two aliens were eating some reels of film. "Isn't this the best meal you've ever had?" said one. "No," said the other. "I liked the book better."

When did the cow jump over the moon?
    When she was in the moo-d.

Val: Would you rather have a Saturnian attack you, or a Plutonian?
Sal: I'd rather have the Saturnian attack the Plutonian.

Teacher: Class, tell me how fast light travels.
Student: The same way slow light does.

What did the alien say when he saw the Russian cosmonauts land on the moon?
    Nothing. Aliens can't speak Russian.

What phone system is used in outer space?
    E.T. and T.

A Martian landed on earth on a goodwill mission. When he met the president, he took a deep bow. One of the president's advisers then whispered to the Martian, "You must not bow before the president." "Oh, please forgive me," the Martian replied. "I didn't know it was his turn."

What's big, green, and eats peanuts?
  A Martian elephant.

How did the sailor know there wasn't a man in the moon?
  He'd been to sea.

Moe: I just read a real down-to-earth story.
Joe: What was it about?
Moe: The last space flight.

Why does a baby alien walk softly?
  Because he can't walk, hardly.

Why did the astronaut take a nap in the spaceship?
  She wanted to get some shuttle-eye.

Where does the sun belong?
  In the Hall of Flame.

Martian: Doctor, I think I'm a dog.
Doctor: How long has this been going on?
Martian: Ever since I was a puppy.

1st astronaut: Last night I dreamed I was in Paris.
2nd astronaut: That's nothing. Last night I dreamed
    I won a free ticket on the next space shuttle to
    Pluto.
1st astronaut: Well, why didn't you invite me?
2nd astronaut: I tried to, but your wife said you
    were in Paris.

*Why did the alien turn away when he saw the moth
cry?*
  He couldn't bear to see a moth bawl.

*What did the alien say when she held down the
pig?*
  "I won't let you up till you say oinkel." (uncle)

Harry: What's the difference between a poet and an
    astronomer?
Barry: I don't know, what?
Harry: A poet tries to get his head into the heavens;
    an astronomer tries to get the heavens into his
    head.

Why is an astronaut like a quarterback?
  They both want to make successful touchdowns.

What tiny insects are found on space shuttles?
  Astro-gnats.

Pam: I think I might be going to the moon.
Sam: What makes you say that?
Pam: My dad told me that if I misbehaved one
more time, he'd send me into orbit.

1st Martian: Which would you prefer to eat, a juicy
steak or a shooting star?
2nd Martian: I'd prefer the shooting star, because
it's meteor. (meatier)

*What happened when the alien boarding house
blew up?*
Roomers flew. (rumors)

How did the alien make a dollar fast?
She nailed it to a table.

Terry: Did the teacher really say your voice was out
of this world?
Perry: No, she said it was unearthly.

Where does a witch keep her flying saucer?
In the broom closet.

*How did the girl alien hold onto her boyfriend's
love?*
By not returning it.

1st Martian: Did you hear the joke about the picture
    window?
2nd Martian: No, tell me.
1st Martian: Never mind, you'd see right through it.

*What happened when the alien couldn't tell the
difference between cold cream and putty?*
    All her windows fell out.

*What did the alien do when his wife made him a
marble cake?*
    He took it for granite.

1st alien: Did you hear about the Venusian surgeon
    who stopped drinking?
2nd alien: No.
1st alien: Now he's a dry doc.

*What's red and white on the outside and green and
lumpy on the inside?*
    A can of cream of alien soup.

Boy Martian: Here's a present for you.
Girl Martian: How lovely! Thank you.
Boy Martian: Yes, I made it myself with my own
    five hands.

Why did the astronaut tiptoe past the medicine cabinet?

He didn't want to wake the sleeping pills.

Why did the Neptunian break up with his girlfriend?

He needed more space.

What do you call an alien who lends his tools to a neighbor?

A saw loser.

Why isn't the moon rich?

Because it spends its quarters getting full.

What did the alien gardener say when his flowers wouldn't bloom?
   "Upsadaisy!"

What zone do aliens park in?
   The Twilight Zone.

What is the secret of space travel?
   Don't look down.

Mother: I think our daughter is going to be an astronaut.
Father: Why is that?
Mother: I talked to her teacher today, and she said Susie is just taking up space.

Why did the boy grow up to be an astronaut?
   Because everyone said he was up to no earthly good.

A woman saw a Neptunian walking down a city street carrying bread and butter. "What are you doing?" she asked the Neptunian. "Oh, I'm looking for the traffic jam," replied the Neptunian.

Passenger: May I have a ticket to the moon?
Ticket seller: I'm sorry, the moon is full just now.

Teacher: Class, where did the rocks on the moon
come from?
Student: From a comet.
Teacher: And where is the comet now?
Student: It went back to get more rocks.

Where does an astronaut keep his handkerchief?
In an air pocket.

Reporter: What made you change professions from
an astronaut to a sky diver?
Astronaut: A four-engine rocket ship with four dead
engines.

*Why didn't the two astronauts want to travel faster
than sound?*
Because they wanted to be able to talk to each
other.

How can you tell a Martian from a grape?
Jump up and down on it. If you don't get any
wine, it's a Martian.

What do you call the border of an otter territory?
The Otter Limits.

Why did the scientist paint his spaceship gold?
He had a gilt complex. (guilt)

Why did the astronaut sleep under her spaceship?
  She wanted to wake up oily in the morning.

Knock, knock.
Who's there?
Fire engine.
Fire engine who?
Fire engine one and get ready for blast-off!

How do you make a Martian stew?
  Keep it waiting for a few hours.

1st astronaut: Joe quit being an astronaut to
     become a traffic cop.
2nd astronaut: Is he happy?
1st astronaut: I think so. He's always whistling while
     he works.

Passenger: Your timetable is no good! The
     spaceships are always late.
Conductor: Think of it this way, you wouldn't know
     they were late if it weren't for the timetable.

Astronaut: I was just bitten on the leg by an alien.
Doctor: Did you put anything on it?
Astronaut: No. He liked it the way it was.

Why did the alien take a hammer to bed with her?
  She wanted to hit the hay.

*What would you do if an eight-foot alien sat in front
of you at the movies?*
  Miss most of the movie.

Space police: We clocked you speeding at 155,000
    miles an hour.
Alien: That's ridiculous. I haven't even been out for
    an hour.

Girl: Mom, I'm going to watch the eclipse.
Mother: OK, dear. But don't stand too close.

1st alien: If you were in line at a ticket window, and the Martian in front of you was buying a ticket to Pluto, and the Venusian behind you was buying a ticket to Jupiter, where would you be going?
2nd alien: I don't know.
1st alien: Well, if you don't know where you're going, why are you in line?

Why did the silly astronaut bring glue with him?
In case he saw daybreak.

Which planet is best for measuring temperature?
Mercury.

What do space explorers argue about more than anything else?
Who gets to sit next to the window.

How did the astronaut describe her first trip to the moon?
"Out of this world."

Which planet is most sure of itself?
Saturn-ly. (Certainly)

Why did the alien go to the doctor?
 She had varicose Vein-us. (Venus)

What helps the Starship Enterprise run?
 Spock plugs.

Alien: If you want to stay on this planet, earthling,
 you must take smart pills.
Astronaut: Ground control didn't give me any smart
 pills.
Alien: Oh, very well. I can sell you some for $200.
Astronaut: OK. Here's the money.
Alien: Thank you, earthling. Here are your pills.
Astronaut: Hey! These look like jelly beans!
Alien: See? You're getting smarter already.

What gets larger the more you take away from it?
 A black hole.

A Neptunian was invited to a party on Pluto and
was running late. She went up to a Plutonian and
said, "Can you tell me what time it is? I was invited
to a party and my watch isn't going." The Plutonian
said, "That's a shame. Why wasn't your watch
invited?"

1st astronaut: Your spaceship is at the door.
2nd astronaut: Yes, I hear it knocking.

1st astronaut: What would you say if 45 aliens jumped out at you?

2nd astronaut (thinking): I give up.

1st astronaut: That's correct, but you'd have to say it faster than that.

Alien (on the phone): Fire department? Hurry! My spaceship is on fire!

Earth fireman: How do we get to you?

Alien: Oh, gracious. Don't you have those big red trucks anymore?

Why did the Alpha Centaurian feed money to the cow?

She wanted to get rich milk.

What happened to the astronaut who swallowed his spoon?
　He couldn't stir.

　A flying saucer landed at a gas station on earth. An alien got out and observed the gas pumps for a couple of hours. When he returned to his planet, his superiors asked him what he had to report. "I don't think we have much to fear from earthlings," the alien responded. "They spend all day standing around with their fingers in their ears."

What did the police do when a hundred hares escaped from the space zoo?
　They combed the area.

Venusian: I just arrived here on earth. I need a
　　　room for the night.
Hotel clerk: Single?
Venusian: Yes, but I'm engaged to be married
　　　soon.

1st alien: What's the difference between an
　　　earthling and a mattababy?
2nd alien: What's a mattababy?
1st alien: Nothing, I'm fine. What's the matter with
　　　you?

What does a Plutonian eat?
  Plutatoes.

What does an android frog say?
  "Robot . . . robot . . . robot."

Martian: Doctor, I need help. Ever since I've been
    on earth I think I'm a dog.
Doctor: Come in my office and lie down on this
    couch.
Martian: I can't. I'm not allowed on the furniture.

A Venusian attended several piano concerts while
she was on earth. Before she left the planet, she
wanted to take a piano with her. She went into a
music store and asked the clerk, "Do you carry
pianos?" "Not if I can help it," the clerk answered.
"They're too heavy."

Hal: Did you hear about the astronaut who went on a coconut diet?
Sal: No. Did she lose weight?
Hal: No, but you should see her climb trees!

Two aliens were on a camping trip on earth when they were attacked by mosquitoes. They hid under a mosquito net to avoid being bitten. Later on one of the aliens saw a swarm of lightning bugs headed their way. "Look out!" he told the other alien. "They're coming after us with flashlights now!"

What do you get when you cross a rabbit with a spaceship?
A space vehicle that's used only for short hops.

An Alpha Centaurian landed on earth and crashed into a rich man's car. The man was very angry and began yelling. The Centaurian shrugged and said, "Well, that's the way the Mercedes Benz." (bends)

Astronaut: Doctor, I swallowed a clock during last month's space flight.
Doctor: Goodness! Why didn't you come to me sooner?
Astronaut: I didn't want to alarm anyone.

What did the alien say to the gardener?
   "Take me to your weeder."

What do you get when you cross a 200-pound chicken with a 500-pound silly Martian?
   The biggest dumb cluck in the universe.

What did the android say when he saw the wire trash basket?
   "Put some clothes on! You'll catch your death of cold!"

Attractive alien: May I try on that outfit in the window?
Shop owner: I wish you would. It would be great for business.

An astronaut opened the refrigerator in his space shuttle and saw a rabbit inside.
Astronaut: What are you doing in there?
Rabbit: This is a Westinghouse, isn't it?
Astronaut: Yes, it is.
Rabbit: Well, I'm westing.

1st astronaut: I heard you buried your spaceship. Why?
2nd astronaut: Well, the pistons were shot and the battery died.

An Alpha Centaurian landed on a Florida beach.
He took out a pair of skis.

Sunbather: What are you doing with those skis?
There's no snow on the beach.

Centaurian: That's all right. It's coming with the rest
of my luggage.

Teacher: Class, which is closer to us, California or
the moon?

Student: The moon.

Teacher: I'm afraid you're wrong.

Student: No, I'm not. I can see the moon from
here. I can't see California.

Spaceship driver: Look outside and tell me if my
    blinker is working.
Passenger: Yes-no-yes-no-yes-no-yes-no.

An insurance salesman was talking to a Martian
who had landed on earth.
Salesman: If you want to stay on this planet, you
    should buy accident insurance.
Martian: Really? Why?
Salesman: I'll tell you why. A few days ago I sold a
    policy to this one gentleman. The very next
    day he broke his neck, and we paid him
    $100,000. You might be as lucky as he was!

*What's the difference between a dog with fleas and
an astronaut waiting on a launching pad?*
    One is going to itch, the other is itching to go.

*Why did the Venusian put her hand in front of her
mouth when she sneezed?*
    To catch her breath.

Teacher: Please use the word "astronavigation" in
    a sentence.
Student: OK. What does "astronavigation" mean?

A Martian prisoner escaped from jail and fled to earth. When he landed, he ran out of his spaceship yelling, "I'm free! I'm free!" A little girl saw him and said, "So what? I'm four."

A Martian walked into a malt shoppe and ordered a banana split with chocolate syrup and chopped nuts. The worker made one for the Martian. "I notice you've been staring at me," said the Martian to the worker. "I suppose you think it's strange that a Martian comes into your shop and orders a banana split with chocolate syrup and nuts." The worker replied, "Not really. I like banana splits that way myself."

Teacher: What are you drawing?
Student: The surface of Pluto.
Teacher: But no one knows what the surface of Pluto looks like.
Student: They will when I'm done.

Reporter: And how do you like riding in a space shuttle?
Astronaut: Oh, I have no room to complain.

Why couldn't the crescent moon do its laundry?
Because it had run out of quarters.

Janie: Yesterday I saw a star with a tail.
Lanie: You mean you saw a comet?
Janie: No, I saw Lassie.

1st Martian: Is this the other side of the crater?
2nd Martian: No, it's over there.
1st Martian: That's funny. The Martian over there
    said it was over here.

1st alien: I wish I had the money to buy an
    elephant.
2nd alien: What do you want with an elephant?
1st alien: Nothing. I just want the money.

1st astronaut: I just got a new radio for the space
    shuttle. Last night I got Mexico on it.
2nd astronaut: That's nothing. I just opened my
    window and got Chile.

Why wasn't the astronaut very smart?
    He went to the Naval Training Center to have his
belly button trained.

1st astronaut: If your space shuttle was flying
    toward Pluto, what would you see on your
    right hand?
2nd astronaut: My fingers.

What's a person on roller skates to an alien monster?
    Meals on wheels.

Brother (pointing up at sky): That star up there is
    Mars.
Sister: Then that star over there must be Pa's.

Where did the Martian stop for gas?
    At the nearest space station.

What is the difference between sunrise and sunset?
    A day.

A space pilot was offering rides in his rocket ship for $10. He was trying to convince a young couple to go up with him. They had never been up in a rocket ship before. "C'mon, it'll be fun," the pilot said. "If you promise to be quiet and not be backseat drivers, I'll let you both ride for free." The husband and wife agreed. The rocket ship went up, did some fancy loops, and came back down again. The pilot turned to the husband and said, "You did very well for your first flight. I didn't hear a peep out of you!" "Well, it wasn't easy," said the husband. "I almost said something back there when my wife fell out."

A Venusian landed on earth. She was curious about earth movies, so she went to a movie theater.
Venusian: I'd like another ticket, please.
Ticket seller: That's the third one you've bought for this show. Why are you buying so many?
Venusian: Because that man inside the theater keeps tearing them up.

What do you call a crazy space explorer?
    An astronut.

What's an alien's favorite candy?
    Mars bars.

Why did the Plutonian go to the beach at night?
  She wanted to get a moontan.

Where did the nutmeg alien come from?
  Outer spice.

What did the astronaut say when she was asked about UFOs?
  "No comet."

Astronaut: We just landed in the middle of the
    Atlantic Ocean. Please send a rescue crew.
Ground control: Capsize?
Astronaut: Oh, about 14 inches around.

What's a Martian's favorite old song?
  "The Moonlight Sonata."

What do you get when you cross a large alien with a computer?
  A 500-pound genius.

What steps would you take if an alien monster was chasing you?
  Long ones.

Where is the planet Pluto?
  Out of this world.

Muffy: What's the difference between a Martian and a cantaloupe?

Buffy: I don't know.

Muffy: Boy, I'd hate to send you to the store for cantaloupes.

Bud: What do you get if you cross an alien with a parrot?

Jud: I don't know, but you'd better give it a cracker when it asks for one.

Tad: Wow, it says here that we've made amazing progress in space travel in the last 10 years.
Brad: Yes, now we're only 50 years behind the comic books.

A Martian ordered an ice-cream sundae at a restaurant.
Martian: Waiter, there's a fly in my ice cream.
Waiter: Serves it right. Let it freeze to death!

1st tourist: The acoustics in this new space station are fabulous, aren't they?
2nd tourist: What?

Why are robots so fearless?
Because they have nerves of steel.

Where do otters come from?
Otter space.

What did the Martian say when he saw the keys on the grand piano?
"Take me to your dentist."

What do you call it when the earth rotates backward?
Revearth.

1st astronaut: I saw my old boss the other day. She
    has really gained in years.
2nd astronaut: Really?
1st astronaut: Yes. But it's OK. They're light years.

Knock, knock!
Who's there?
Athena.
Athena who?
Athena shooting star last night.

1st astronaut: Will you join me on the moon?
2nd astronaut: Why, are you coming apart?

Teacher: What is the shape of the earth?
Student: It's square.
Teacher: No, that's wrong. It's round.
Student: Then why do tourists travel to the four
    corners of the world?

*What did the silly astronaut say when he put his
tooth under his pillow and found a dollar the next
day?*
    "I have buck teeth!"

What kind of knots do you find in outer space?
    Astronauts.

Did you hear about the Martian who made a new boomerang?
He went crazy trying to throw the old one away.

What do you get when you cross a rocket ship with a wizard?
A flying sorcerer.

What astronaut wears the largest helmet?
The one with the largest head.

What time is it when a 500-pound alien sits on a satellite?
Time to get a new satellite.

Teacher: Did your parents help you with these
astronomy questions?
Student: No, I got them wrong all by myself.

1st Saturnian: We should be able to land on earth
soon. There's Egypt, and there's the Nile River.
2nd Saturnian: Excellent. We hit the Nile right on
the head.

Who won the alien beauty contest?
Nobody.

How did Mary and her little lamb get to Mars?
  By rocket sheep.

Mother alien: Who was that on the phone?
Son alien: Just somebody who said it was long
    distance from Pluto, and I said it sure was!

Reporter: Didn't the loss of heat bother you when
    you went up into space?
Astronaut: No. I just threw the thermometer out of
    the space shuttle and watched the temperature
    drop.

What's another name for a space scientist?
  A night watchman.

1st scientist: Why did the germ cross the
      microscope?
2nd scientist: To get to the other slide.

*What did the young Martian say when she got a
bad moonburn and began peeling?*
   "Five years old and wearing out already."

When can you see through an astronaut?
   When he has a pane in his stomach. (pain)

Why is the weather forecast like a baby?
   Because it is always being changed.

Andy: There's a parrot on the moon that lays
      square eggs.
Sandy: No kidding! Does it talk?
Andy: Yes, but it says only one word.
Sandy: What's that?
Andy: Ouch!

1st astronaut: Can you telephone from a satellite?
2nd astronaut: Sure. Anyone can tell a phone from
      a satellite. The satellite is the one that doesn't
      have a dial tone.

How does the sun affect weight?
   By making the daylight.

What's tall, black, and takes your order?
  Darth Waiter.

Jo: Well, this year I failed every class except
      astronomy.
Bo: How did you keep from failing astronomy?
Jo: I didn't take it.

What's a race car driver's favorite film?
  Steer Wars.

*Did you hear the joke about the astronaut who had
celery sticks in her ears?*
  Never mind, she didn't hear it either.

How do you put a space monster to sleep?
  Rock-et.

Tina: I heard the astronauts found some bones on
    the moon.
Gina: Gee, I guess the cow didn't make it after all.

A Neptunian was visiting a museum in New York City. "And this hideous thing, I suppose," she told the curator, "is what you earthlings call modern art?" "No," said the curator. "That is a mirror."

1st Martian: I know a restaurant in space where we
    can eat dirt cheap.
2nd Martian: I don't care how cheap it is. Who
    wants to eat dirt?

Just before a Venusian left earth, she went into a hardware store to buy some wallpaper. "I want something pretty," she told the clerk. "Do you have any wallpaper that has daisies on it?" "Yes, we do," answered the clerk. "Can I put it on myself?" asked the Venusian. "Yes, ma'am," said the clerk, "but I think it would look better on the wall."

Freddy: Did you hear about the new invention that
    actually lets astronauts see through the walls of
    a space shuttle?
Teddy: No. What's it called?
Freddy: A window.

Passenger: Excuse me, how long will the next
spaceship to the moon be?
Ticket seller: Oh, about 500 feet, ma'am.

*What did the elephant astronaut say into the
comlink?*
   "Tusking, one, two, three . . . tusking, one, two,
three."

Boy: I want to study the stars.
Girl: Why don't you just get a map of Hollywood
then?

What do aliens invest in?
   Moon-icipal bonds.

Teacher: How do we know the earth is round?
Students: Why are you asking us? We never said it
was!

Clara: Did you hear about the Venusian king who
owned many castles and became very rude
when he got rid of all of them?
Sara: No.
Clara: He lost all his manors.

Where did the alien trial take place?
   In moon-icipal court.

A Venusian traveling through the U.S. stopped at a farm in the midwest. He saw an old man sitting in the sun holding a stick with a piece of string tied to it. "What is that in your hand, earthling?" asked the Venusian. "It's a weather gauge," answered the old man. "How can it possibly work?" the Venusian said. "Well," the old man said, "when it swings back and forth, it's windy, and when it gets wet, it's raining."

What happened to the alien who ate the electric company?
She was in shock for a week.

Space police: Did you see a Martian take this road a little while ago?
Bystander: No, sir, the road is still there.

Why did the astronaut blast off at noon?
Because 12 o'clock is time for launch.

1st Venusian: We should be able to land on earth soon. There is the Pacific Ocean!
2nd Venusian: Look at all that water!
1st Venusian: Yes, and that's only the top!

What does a magician perform in space?
  Star tricks.

What is the center of gravity?
  The letter V.

Three astronauts were standing under one small umbrella. There was thunder and lightning everywhere. Why didn't they get wet?
  It wasn't raining.

1st Martian: English food must be fattening.
2nd Martian: What makes you say that?
1st Martian: This earth paper says that a woman in London lost 500 pounds.

Who was a famous musician and space explorer?
  Bach Rogers.

What happened when the musician Bach Rogers took too many baths?
  He began writing soap operas.

Martian king: What did you bring back from the planet earth?
Martian explorer: Well, Your Highness, my partner and I went on an African safari and brought back this stuffed lion.
Martian king: It's quite magnificent. What is it stuffed with?
Martian explorer: My partner.

A tour guide was showing the awesome rings of Saturn to a group of travelers. "Here are some spectacles you never forget," she said. "Can you get me a pair?" one tourist said. "I'm always forgetting mine."

1st astronaut: Hand me the updoc over there.
2nd astronaut: What's updoc?
1st astronaut: Nothing. What's up with you?

Two Martians were studying a mailbox and a fire alarm.
1st Martian: What are these things?
2nd Martian: I'm not sure. This blue thing doesn't say a word, but if you touch this red contraption, it yells its head off!

Who's a Martian's favorite actress?
  Marilyn Moonroe.

Astronaut: Doctor, ever since we came back from that space flight a month ago, my partner thinks she's a chicken.
Doctor: Why didn't you come to me sooner?
Astronaut: Well, we needed the eggs.

Why is the light from the moon like illegal liquor?
  They're both moonshine.

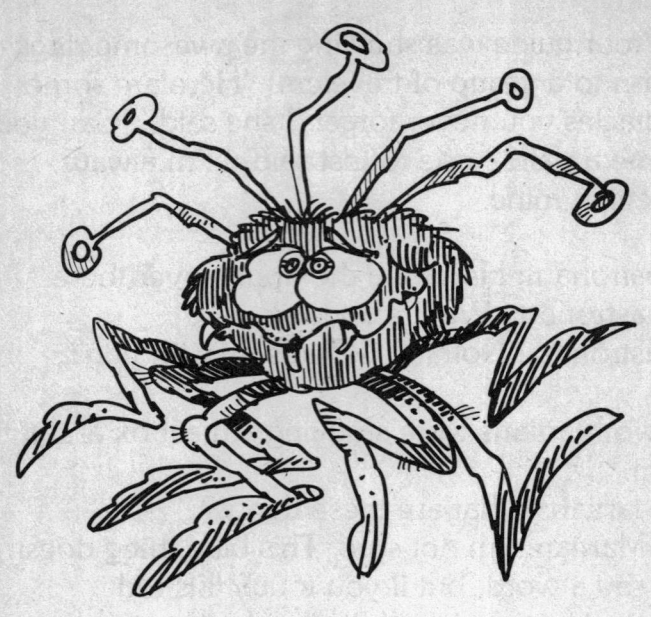

What do you call a crazy alien insect?
  A lunar-tic.

Biff: Why do aliens have square shoulders?
Cliff: Because they eat lots of cereal.
Biff: How can cereal give them square shoulders?
Cliff: It isn't the cereal, it's the boxes.

What did the baby planet say when it broke out of orbit?
  "Look, Ma, no gravities."

Where does an astronaut go when she's hungry?
  To the launcheonette counter.

Where do they keep prisoners in outer space?
  In solar cells.

What did the Martian order for dinner?
  Filet of solar.

Why did the astronaut go to court?
  To file a space suit.

1st alien: You must think I'm the perfect idiot.
2nd alien: No. After all, nobody's perfect.

  Two aliens were watching a space flight on TV.
1st alien: Boy, I'd hate to be up 10,000 miles in
      space in a rocket ship.
2nd alien: I'd hate to be up there without one.

How did the astronaut get to the planet of the apes?
  He took the banana boat.

Hal: I got a job flipping the switches at Cape
      Kennedy.
Cal: Is it a steady job?
Hal: Oh, it's sort of on and off.

What's an alien's favorite Italian dish?
  Space-ghetti and moonballs.

Why did the alien go to the health spa?
  To get a spacial.

Phil: My mom is in the aerospace industry.
Gil: Oh, yeah? How's business?
Phil: It's up in the air.

1st parent: My husband and I are sending our kids
    to space camp this summer.
2nd parent: Do they need a vacation?
1st parent: No. We do.

1st astronaut: We're going faster than the speed of
    sound.
2nd astronaut: What did you say?

Nan: Pretend you're being chased by a dozen scary
    aliens. What would you do?
Fran: I'd stop pretending.

Why did the alien poke a hole in the carpet?
    She wanted to see the floor show.

Why did the astronaut go to the planetarium?
    To see an all-star production.

Venusian king: What was the richest country you
    found on earth?
Venusian explorer: Ireland, because its capital is
    always Dublin.

Martian king: Agent Voltan, why does the Statue of
    Liberty stand in New York harbor?
Martian agent: Because it can't sit down, sir.

1st astronaut: Did you hear about the astronaut
   who became a tree surgeon?
2nd astronaut: No, was he successful?
1st astronaut: No, he kept falling out of his patients.

*If an alien smashed a clock, would he be convicted
of killing time?*
   Not if the clock struck first.

1st astronaut: How's the radio working?
2nd astronaut: It isn't working, it's playing.

*How do you calculate the atomic weight of lunar
rocks?*
   Atom up.

Why didn't the astronaut like to travel?
   He always got spacesick.

An alien landed on earth. She asked several
people what time it was. The last person she asked
told her it was six o'clock. "Oh, no!" the alien said.
"What's wrong?" the person asked. "All day I've
been asking everyone what time it is," the alien
said, "and everyone's given me a different answer!"

Boy android: Excuse me, but are you unattached?
Girl android: No, I'm just put together sloppily.

Professor: You must make successful landings if you want to graduate from astronaut school.
Student: How many do I need to make?
Professor: All of them.

Why did the Martian go to the beauty salon?
   To get a moonicure.

How do aliens send important messages?
   By spacial delivery.

Why is an alien like a family who has cable television?
   Both watch satellite TV.

What's the best way to keep a dirty alien from smelling?
    Hold its nose.

What are little girl aliens made of?
    Sugar and space.

How does a Martian make a large purchase?
    He uses a crater card.

How can you tell when you've gone through the Milky Way?
    When it's past-your-eyes. (pasteurized)

Which is heavier, a half moon or a full moon?
    A half moon, because a full moon is lighter.

Why are western prairies so flat?
    Because the sun sets on them every night.

Why did the Venusian win the election?
    He had the crater majority of votes.

What do you call a spaceship out of control?
    A shooting star.

Why did the alien wear two pairs of pants when he went golfing?
In case he got a hole-in-one.

What do aliens read by?
  Starlight.

What happened when the electricity went out on the spaceship?
  The astronauts sat 'til light. (satellite)

1st astronaut: What did you think of your first meal
      on the moon?
2nd astronaut: The food was good, but the place
      lacked atmosphere.

Art: Can you name 10 aliens in 10 seconds?
Bart: Nine Venusians and a Martian.

What happened when the alien monster ate the house?
   He got homesick.

1st astronaut: Those are very loud socks you're wearing.
2nd astronaut: Yes, they keep me awake during the space flight.

1st Martian kid: What does your mom do for a headache?
2nd Martian kid: She sends me outside to play.

Why was the astronaut having a snack?
   He was on his launch break.

How do you arrange a trip through space?
   Planet. (plan it)

Passenger: Can I take this spaceship to Jupiter?
Conductor: No, ma'am, it's much too heavy.

1st Plutonian: Can I sit on your right hand?
2nd Plutonian: You can for now, but I may need it later to eat with.

1st Martian: I went to a big fire sale when I was on
    earth.
2nd Martian: What did you buy?
1st Martian: Four big fires.

Why did the alien take a ruler to bed?
    To see how long she slept.

What TV show describes a confused alien?
    "Lost in Space."

What do aliens use when they shave?
    Laser blades.

How many Martians can you put in an empty sack?
    One. After that the sack isn't empty.

Why are Martians so polite?
    They don't want to alienate anyone.

Benny: What do you get when you cross a puppy
    with a 200-pound alien?
Jenny: I don't know, but I hope it can't get through
    the dog door.

What's the last word in rockets?
    Fire!

What do all Martians in the universe do at the same time?
　Grow older.

Why did the alien take his date off the planet?
　He wanted to talk to her space-to-space.

Mission control: What do you have to report?
Astronaut: Well, here's the good news: there is life
　　on Jupiter. Here's the bad news: we owe them
　　rent.

What do aliens race on in space?
　Star tracks.

What time is it when a huge alien walks up to you?
  Time to run!

What did the girl Saturnian say to the boy Saturnian on their date?
  "There's a beautiful earth out tonight."

Astronaut: I don't feel so good after that last space flight.
Doctor: What are your symptoms?
Astronaut: My ears are plugged up, my nose is dripping, and my chest is clogged.
Doctor: You don't need a doctor, you need a plumber.

Teacher: If you see the sun on one side of the earth and the moon on the other, where do you see the stars?
Student: On TV.

What happened when the zombie went up in space?
  He experienced zero grave-ity.

1st astronaut: Why do you have your leg in a cast?
2nd astronaut: I broke my leg in two places last week.
1st astronaut: Well, you shouldn't go to those places anymore.

A man spotted a Martian looking at the sidewalk.

Man: Excuse me, what are you looking for?

Martian: I dropped my wallet over on Main Street.

Man: But why are you looking here? This isn't Main Street!

Martian: I know, but the light is better here.

1st astronaut: Our work is too stressful. I'm thinking of quitting and going to work in a watch factory. That job would be much easier.

2nd astronaut: Why?

1st astronaut: All I would do is sit around all day and make faces.

Why did the Martian take the bus?
  Because his spaceship was in the shop.

Pat: Hey, did you hear about the astronaut who blasted off on Friday and came back four days later on Friday?

Nat: That's impossible.

Pat: No, it's not. His spaceship's name is Friday.

Why didn't the astronauts show up for work on a holiday?
  It wasn't NASA-cessary.

What do you call two aliens in love?
  Earthstruck.

Two aliens landed on a corner and started arguing about the traffic light. "I saw her first!" said one alien. "So what?" said the other. "I'm the one she winked at."

What do you call a bald head on a space explorer? The Astrodome.

Why did the asteroid step into the bathtub?
  It was going to take a meteor shower.

Astronaut: After that last space mission my ear rings
    constantly.
Doctor: Try getting an unlisted ear.

Why don't spaceships have bucket seats?
  Because not every astronaut has the same size
bucket.

  An alien walked into an earth restaurant that
served southern food.
Alien: I'll have the grits, please.
Waiter: Hominy, madame?
Alien: Oh, at least a whole bowlful.

Tad: Did you hear about the nuclear physicist who
    was overworked?
Brad: No, what about her?
Tad: She had too many ions in the fire.

1st astronaut: What are you doing?
2nd astronaut: I'm writing a letter to myself.
1st astronaut: You're crazy. What does the letter
    say?
2nd astronaut: I don't know. I won't get it till
    tomorrow.

A rocket ship blasted off, carrying the first passengers to Mars. The passengers heard a voice over the loudspeaker: "Welcome aboard, ladies and gentlemen. This is your automatic pilot speaking. You are riding on the most sophisticated rocket ship ever built. Just sit back and relax. Nothing can go wrong . . . go wrong . . . go wrong . . ."

Venusian: Earthling, I hear milk baths are good for the skin. I would like to buy 12 gallons of milk.
Milkman: Would you like it pasteurized?
Venusian: No, up to my knees will be fine.

Why did the space explorer go to the doctor?
To get an astrophysical.

What do you call an asteroid that stamps envelopes?
A postage meteor.

Teacher: Who can name a deadly poison?
Student: Space exploration!
Teacher: Space exploration?
Student: Yes. One drop and you're dead.

What happened when the boy asteroid saw the girl asteroid?
He wanted to meteor. (meet her)

Why did the Martians visit Washington, DC?
  They wanted to see the Washington Moonument.

1st alien: When astronauts visit my planet, they
    come to see me.
2nd alien: Yes, you sure are a sight.

What's an astronaut's favorite place for a tropical
vacation?
  NASA (Nassau), the Bahamas.

What's green, weighs 1,000 pounds, and has eight wheels?

An alien on roller skates.

What do restaurants serve in space?
  Spaghetti and meteorballs.

What happened to the insane Martian?
  He got thrown into the lunar bin.

Girl alien: Now that we're engaged, I hope you'll
    give me a ring.
Boy alien: Sure. What's your number?

Martian mother: Doctor, my son just swallowed a
    ray gun. What should I do?
Doctor: Don't point him at anyone.

*What happened when the astronauts decided to
settle their case out of court?*
  They went into orbit-ration. (arbitration)

What layer isn't found on a cake?
  The ozone layer.

1st astronaut: I see spots every time I go on a space
    flight.
2nd astronaut: Have you seen a doctor?
1st astronaut: No, just spots.

What do you call a beautiful garden on the moon?
  A garden of unearthly delights.

1st astronaut: I can lift an alien with one hand.
2nd astronaut: You're lying.
1st astronaut: Give me an alien with one hand, and
    I'll prove it.

1st Martian: My dad thinks I'm too thin.
2nd Martian: Why?
1st Martian: He always says he can see right
    through me.

1st astronaut: I finally went to see a doctor about
    my forgetfulness.
2nd astronaut: What did he do?
1st astronaut: He made me pay in advance.

What's the best way to drive an alien baby buggy?
    Tickle its feet.

What did the astronaut's children bring to school?
    Their launch money.

Alien: Is your water supply healthy here, earthling?
Man: Yes, we use only well water.

A hungry alien was in the mood for shellfish. He
walked into a restaurant and asked, "Do you serve
crabs here?" "Certainly, sir," the hostess answered,
"we serve anyone."

Why did the mother knit her astronaut son three socks after he had been in space for a year?
Because he wrote that he had grown another foot.

What two beaux could the pretty alien not get rid of?
Her elbows.

Why did the Neptunian swallow an umbrella?
   She wanted to put something away for a rainy day.

What time was it when the hungry alien ate the postmaster?
   Ate P.M.

What did the alien take when he was run down?
The license plate number of the spaceship that hit him.

If an alien is born on Mercury, grows up on Venus, moves to Saturn, and dies on Pluto, what is he?
Dead.

Three aliens fell into the water, but only two got their hair wet. How?
One of them was bald.

An alien spaceship flew to earth and landed on top of a milk bottling factory. One of the aliens got out and saw all the milk bottles. "Attention, everyone," she announced to the other crew members, "we have landed on a cow's nest."

Martian leader: What did you bring back from
 earth?
Martian pilot: I brought this horseshoe. It is
 supposed to mean good luck.
Martian leader: Well, it may mean good luck for
 you, but some poor earth horse is walking
 around in his socks right now.

What keeps the moon in the sky?
Its beams.

What is a pie in the sky?
  A flying saucer.

What do you call an alien who speaks several languages?
  An alien with many tongues.

What time is it if you divide the moon between four aliens?
  A quarter to one.

What fish do they serve on space shuttles?
  Flying fish.

An alien family landed on earth and was invited to the White House for dinner along with several other aliens. After they left the White House, the father alien asked his child, "Did you thank the president for the dinner?" "No," answered the child. "The alien in front of me thanked him, and the president said, 'Don't mention it.' So I didn't."

Space police: I pulled you over because you were speeding. May I see your license?
Spaceship driver: How can I show you my license when people like you keep taking it away from me?

Why did the silly astronaut put the cake out into the freezing cold of space?
  She wanted icing on her cake.

Why did the astronaut sit down to eat?
  It was launch time.

1st astronaut: Did you hear the joke about the
    chocolate cake?
2nd astronaut: No, tell me.
1st astronaut: Forget it, it's too rich.

  An astronaut landed on Mars and noticed that an alien was following him and staring at him. "Why are you staring at me?" he demanded of the alien. "I'm the food inspector," the alien replied.

What snack does a rocket mechanic like best?
  Assorted nuts.

What do you call low-calorie aging?
  Light years.

  Two aliens were in an earth restaurant.
1st alien: Should you eat spare ribs with your
    fingers?
2nd alien: I think you should eat your fingers
    separately.

Who was the first western settler?
   The sun.

What happened when the astronaut drank eight colas?
   He burped 7-Up.

What did the Saturnian part with when he left earth?
   A comb.

Astronaut: Doctor, sometimes I wake up thirsty in
      the middle of the night.
Doctor: Next time look under the mattress and find
      the spring.

   Two androids from Jupiter landed on earth. One
of them saw a bubble gum machine and put a coin
in it. "Why are you feeding that kid?" said the other
android, alarmed. "You should ask its mother first."

*What did the Neptunian say when he saw the towel
sticking out of the towel dispenser?*
   "Excuse me, madame, your slip is showing."

*What was the largest planet before Jupiter was
discovered?*
   Jupiter.

*Why did the silly astronaut take a pill that was half
aspirin and half glue?*

She had a splitting headache.

Why did the alien get kicked out of the Marines?
He was rotten to the Corps.

A hungry Plutonian landed on earth and went into a restaurant. "I'll have a hamburger, please," he told the waiter. "With pleasure, ma'am," said the waiter. "No, with tomatoes and pickles," said the Plutonian.

What kind of baby would Mr. and Mrs. Sun have?
A very bright one.

Why did the alien cross the road?
It was the chicken's day off.